I0464016

THE PHOTOGRAPHERS MANIFESTO

A Search for Meaning as a Photographer

Bill Hitz

Hitz MediaCom Corp.
Miami, Florida

To receive updates and news, sign up at
www.photographersmanifesto.com

Like the book on Facebook at
www.facebook.com/photographersmanifesto

ISBN 978-1481167383

Printed in the United States of America

About the Author

Bill Hitz has been a photographer all his life. Living and breathing photography since a very young age, early on he appointed himself curator of his family's photos and home movies which now constitute a beautiful vintage collection. Bill benefited from an advanced education in photography. By age 11 he was spending time in a friend's darkroom, learning the nuances of black and white developing and printing.

Born to a German father and Cuban mother in Mexico City, Bill found himself growing up surrounded by artists and photography enthusiasts. Although only amateur photographers, Bill's parents, Julia and Reinhart, were great enablers, always having movie and photo cameras handy. That started a lifelong relationship with cameras and photographs. Bill's mother, an artist, started as a fashion designer in Cuba, later became a commercial artist in Mexico, and eventually a watercolor artist and instructor in Texas and Virginia.

Another strong influence on Bill was the Hitz family's decades-long friendship with the Brehme family of photographers in Mexico, who were there to beautifully capture many highlights of Hitz family history. Hugo Brehme was a German documentary and landscape photographer who in the early 20th century became well known for photographing much of the pristine Mexican countryside, the towns and the people. He was followed by his son, Arno, and Arno's son, Dennis, who is Bill's contemporary.

Like many of you, Bill has been on a life-long mission to find his personal meaning in photography. The passion developed early in life, but the study of its meaning turned into a lifelong search. This book examines the elements that affect a passionate photographer during a lifetime.

Today Bill divides his time between managing his photography business in South Florida, consulting for creative clients, and mentoring photographers.

Jackie Hitz

A Passion Similar to Love

As a recurring and predictable theme, I read about or hear photographers around the world saying "I picked up a camera" or "[enter name here] put a camera in my hands" when I was [enter age here], and I fell in love with capturing images. For over 100 years, especially after George Eastman made photography available to the masses with Kodak box cameras, the same seemingly miraculous experience has been occurring all over the world. It is not a new digital phenomenon. It has existed as long as there have been cameras and persons vulnerable to the spell. In fact, the same emotional experience has likely happened since early man when the first artists began to depict nature through drawings and paintings.

But why is it that this happens to some people and not to others? I grew up with a sister and a brother, yet I was the only sibling obsessed with the process and art of photography. My father was a major influence. He had a medium format camera and an 8mm movie camera, and I used both freely. He taught me about exposure and light control, and also the value of photographs as historical documents. I still treasure our family albums and images dating back to the 19th century. My mother loved the memories of photographs. She was more of a director, having me and my father document our family life. To this day, neither my brother nor my sister ever use a camera -

no point and shoot, no camera phone, nothing - thus negating any genetic theory. For some of us, the visual arts are a different language altogether.

With digital cameras, the pace of new photographers "discovering" the joy and magic of photography has sped up exponentially. This may be due in part to the growth in populations and in part to the fact that snap-shooting with digital cameras, along with easy software, makes photography easier today, more immediately rewarding, and more fun. In less developed countries, affordability and easier access to cameras have empowered many who could not previously afford film, processing and prints. Smartphones have added a new layer of ease and interest, as now most people carry a camera phone all the time, with the ability to upload and share. The days of downloading memory cards to a computer via a cable will one day be a thing of the past. In any case, the learning curve for amateur photographers today is quite different from five years, 20 years and certainly 100 years ago.

Regardless, the mystery of the realization, infatuation, and passion is as similar between those photographers affected as it is between those who catch other interests. Their stories always sound the same. Humans are susceptible to special interest passions, and often the attraction evolves from the experience of a friend, family member or other mentor. Notable popular passions include numerous sports, coins and stamps, guns and hunting, hobbies, cars, aviation, politics, and the list goes on.

Photography is a complex discipline - a craft, a technical process, and an art form. The passion developed is therefore not unlike that of the artist who realizes that she is a painter. Her passion strikes at some point in her life and becomes a life-long obsession. Photographers develop their style, just as painters do. A painter may prefer water colors. A photographer may choose to work primarily with a view camera. The passion may encompass several sub-disciplines.

Some will "discover" photography, develop a passion which will last for a limited time, and then move on to something else. With a phone always in their pocket they will likewise always have a camera with them, but it will no longer be an obsession. They will not consider themselves photographers, just another human being who likes to have some shots from his life experiences. Many will tend to forget they even have an always-there camera in their pocket.

What's the difference between the artist with a lifetime passion and the ordinary person who takes on a hobby and phases out of it later? Are they different internally or is it merely a matter of timelines and duration of the passion? Does it really matter? Is it important to discover now whether you will always be a passionate photographer or do you just let life take you and find out? Maybe we don't really have that choice while we are under the spell of our obsession. Only nature and time will tell.

Why Photograph?

Passions and hobbies come in many forms. Some passions are artistic, others scientific, and others don't fall into either category. A mathematician can be passionate about numbers and formulas, as my father was. A biologist can be obsessed with the science of nature's creatures. A skydiver can eat, sleep and dream about jumping from airplanes. And skydiving teams might argue that their formations are also art, similar to those of Circ du Soleil or Busby Berkeley's kaleidoscope ballets.

Let's not forget the world's biggest passion, which is music. Almost everyone claims to love music, and there are endlessly diverse tastes in music. However, very few develop a burning desire to write music, although many would love to play an instrument, with or without any formal training. Very few can do it well. A self-taught instrument player is not the same as as a musician who has learned formally. Some go to music school, learn to read music, learn to play an instrument, but have no imagination for writing an original song or score. But whether they are creators or interpreters, they have a passion for playing music. Most of us just like to listen to others' music.

Like music, photography can also be a passion of enjoyment without creation. Whether a collector of current or old fine art photographs, or one who buys photography art books or magazines, a passion for photography can exist without ever creating photographs.

To develop photographs based on knowledge of the craft takes considerable study. To create beautiful and unique guitar passages also takes similar dedication.

A key difference between photographing and creating music today is that everyone has a camera in their pocket, but not everyone carries a guitar in their jeans. You can take a guitar to a party when you have created songs or practiced the music of other musicians. Yet you grab your phone-camera off the dresser along with your keys without any care of what aperture means, and no one at the party asks you why you brought a phone camera. Everyone there has a camera, but only one person brings a guitar.

Is the history of your passion important, or should you just go out and express yourself? Perhaps too much knowledge of the past may hinder your ability to create unique works. After all, how can one ever invent a new song when they have all the old music bouncing around in their head? Some would suggest that every chord, every passage of notes has already been used in one song or another. Others would venture that a photograph of everything on earth has already been taken, admired, judged, and relegated to some forgotten web site or album. Only a relatively few images make it into magazines, and even fewer to the walls of galleries, exhibits, or collector's walls.

So why bother? Should we just enjoy the creation process knowing someone else already took that shot? Or should we go deeper and try for a more unique approach? The other side of the argument would suggest that all photographic interpretations are unique, that if you have a workshop with twenty photographers, all shooting the same subjects, no two will produce exactly the same results. Even in such a scenario, not only would the angles be different, but the shooting style would likely vary. Many participants would choose different camera settings. The possibilities for the same shot would be numerous, as they well might be for 100 tourists each day photographing the tower of Pisa and other popular spots on the planet.

When you have a passion for photography, none of it matters. The enjoyment and satisfaction comes from the creative process, from making an image that is yours.

The Passion Within

Passion - it is a word that is popular with "photographic artists". "I'm an artist and I have a passion for photography", one will say. Another will tell you he has "a passion to photograph." Yet another will tell you that it is an uncontrollable urge within her. The passion can take on many forms: passion for the equipment; passion for the subjects; passion for artistic expression; or a combination. Some art collectors may love photographs with a passion, yet they may have no desire to use a camera for artistic purposes. Some persons collect old cameras and never use them.

Let's explore each of the photographer variations.

The first one, declaring himself or herself an artist with a passion for photography, is most likely the one who actually eats, breathes and sleeps obsessed with photography. This type of obsession includes all aspects of photography, including cameras, lenses, certain types of subjects, books and magazines on the subject, perhaps post production work, and certainly their photographs and those of others. They may have young or matured talent, but the obsession easily keeps them buried in their own fort.

The second one has a passion to photograph only. He loves to always have a camera in hand, ready to shoot whatever comes along. The passion is for creating the shot, with little interest in post production. He may not necessarily be a street photographer. He can be a fashion or commercial photographer who has visualized a set or a scene. He could be a portrait photographer who has chosen a perfect outdoor location. Regardless, the pleasure is in the shooting and creating the images. He would prefer to leave the post-production or editing to someone else.

The third one will declare an uncontrollable urge within her. She is obsessed with creating many images and many prints, and hopes to sell them on speculation. She will quit her day job to join the art show circuit, where many potential customers may be found looking for budding artists or new photo decor. She will learn more and more about technique and about her own talent, discovering each year, like most of us, that the work she previously did is inferior to what she is doing now.

There is also the easily found fourth photographer who is more obsessed with the equipment than the work he can create with it. He spends less time taking photographs and working on images, and more time reading and learning about all the new toys that come out each month. He is the one you meet at a photographers' gathering and dazzles you with his knowledge of all the specs of this year's and last year's cameras. He has a passion for photographic equipment, but not necessarily for using it. Some of these photographers may also fantasize about the images they will take, yet never bother with shooting unless they are on vacation or at a family gathering. The rest of their shots are just at home with the kids and pets, but they could just as easily have taken these with their phone camera.

Another extreme of this photographer is one who is obsessed about equipment, but equally interested in using it well. He works with it diligently, calculating his lighting and his camera settings to perfection. He has the best gear he can afford, but he does not feel complete until he has produced the final image.

Another photographer has a passion for her subjects. She loves to compose correctly and expose precisely, but having learned her equipment well, she is more passionate about developing her subjects. To her, the shaping and lighting of her inanimate or live subjects is where the reward is found. Her photographs are satisfying because she directed her subjects, models, clients or products to meet her vision. She pre-visualized the final photograph and made it happen because of her subject management. This is not very different from the mentality of movie directors.

A few photographers are looking for general fulfillment of artistic expression. While they recognize photography as an art, they are less concerned about the medium than about the expression of their ideas. Just as some Renaissance artists either painted or created sculpture depending on the subject and its call for the best medium, some artists may not care whether they use a lens or a sketch pad as long as the choice of tool is the best to complete the work of art. They may carefully consider whether they need an iPhone or a Hasselblad for the job.

There are also the art collectors who have a passion for photography. While some may very well be photographers, others have no use for a camera. They love beautiful photographic art. They decorate their homes and offices accordingly, and perhaps even speculate in the collector market as certain photographers become famous and highly sought after. Some may obsess over certain photographs or types of photography, but they are not necessarily artists themselves. Another type of photography collector has evolved on the Internet, thanks to sites like Pinterest.

Finally, there is also the master printer. Today you can still find master printers who work on and enjoy the art of printing photographs. They dedicate their time to the art and perfection of commercial and fine art prints. They love the final photograph as well as the process of creating it. Some like to shoot their own images. Others do not.

So which categories describe you? Be honest with yourself, and know that you need not be strictly of a single category. Do you find yourself best described as one type of photographer, yet wish you were living a different type?

Does your passion create the inspiration or does your inspiration create your passion? This is a very important point to consider in discovering who you are as a photographer.

Your passion within can take many forms. It can also determine your subject preferences, your choice of photography medium and it can influence your reasons to continue as the photographer that you feel you are.

A Concept Millenniums Old
The Origins of the Passion

Based on archeological and historical findings, it can be concluded with fair certainty that a sense of photography existed in men as far back as the stone ages. While it may have been at first manifested as art on cave walls, and later by more sophisticated illustration methods, such as those found inside the Egyptian pyramids, humans have long had a desire to capture the "image" of things and people that they saw before their eyes. Prehistoric artists, with a limited choice of tools, must have had to pre-visualize what their cave wall painting was to look like. Children learning art today use a similar mental process. Their vision of the image comes before the crayon touches the paper. It is inherent in humans to record their history as seen in their mind and save it to an illustration medium. Photography was just a later technical development of a way to save an image.

By the accepted definition of photography as "writing with light", it may not make sense that humans thousands of years ago visualized the photographic process. But a sense of photography means that they could have imagined that there would be a means by which a realistic image could be captured some day without using brushes. In the meantime they evolved the two-dimensional arts of painting, coloring and sketching. Those were the tools available. By no means should it be interpreted that photographers today somehow consider painting inferior. But compared to the realism of unmodified photography, the illustrative arts are, by their own method, a more abstract and interpretive medium. Photography today has the option to be either an interpretive medium or a recorder of reality and history, a choice not easily available to the painter. Paintings are mostly interpretative, but they can also be realistic, as seen in Renaissance era art.

All inventions have taken time to evolve, including the camera. The first invention devised to produce a live image may well have been an early camera obscura. Some historians will argue that all cameras are cameras obscura, whereas others believe the term only applies to a room or box with a pinhole designed to capture the incoming image stream. Credited by historians to little-known visionary inventors, including first in China in the 5th century BC and later Aristotle in the 4th century AD, among others, these pioneers took a windowless room and drilled a narrow hole in the center of the chosen wall, permitting a small beam of light to come through. The beam of light carried with it the the image of the scene outside. Once inside the room, the light expanded and projected the image onto the opposing wall inside. The first images projected onto the walls of cameras obscura were upside down, reversed left and right, and out of focus. These challenges were surmounted by changing the wall distance and by redirecting the image beam with mirrors. Other discoveries of their time included the fact that a narrower hole creates a brighter image, but a hole too small results in a fuzzy image.

Due to its potential for eventually creating transportable images, the camera obscura was discussed among the scientific community for a long time, but its limited usefulness and value reduced it to a questionable curiosity for most people. The search for development of photographic capture continued in many Western countries, but only a few passionate inventors contributed ideas on how to create a capture medium.

The camera obscura and its evolution into transportable boxes, at first also called camera obscura and later view camera and large format camera, is evidence that a photographer's mentality was evolving even more than a thousand years ago. The historical delay from camera obscura to practical view camera was clearly due to another necessary invention - a practical process to record the image onto something more permanent. In fact, it was not until after 1800 AD that real progress was made in the evolution of capture.

As a side note, today's interest in camera obscura continues in the form of the small pin hole camera. These cameras use film and record images produced through nothing other than a pin hole where a lens would normally be. As with cameras obscura, depth of field is not a problem as the small pin hole results in a very small aperture, and almost all of the scene is in focus.

It is fascinating to think about what may have inspired these unknown historical characters to concern themselves with capturing a live image, especially one that could not be recorded. Instead, history suggests that it is probable that the men interested in the capture process were scientists and visionaries uniquely positioned to appreciate the value of one day being able to record those images.

I would argue that a passion for photography, although quite different from the modern case, existed in those pioneers, and they set the foundation for those future inventors who would eventually find the way to record what was coming into the box. Naturally, to fine tune the camera invention, something better than a pin hole would be necessary. Already studying the relationship between the eye and the image in the brain, camera obscura lenses were developed to improve the method of projecting the image into the box.

The legendary and factual history of photography is international, detailed and very interesting. I encourage all photographers to take time to at least study the highlights. Wikipedia is a good start, but many books on photographic history are also available. Its purpose here is only to relate it to the passion of contemporary photographers. We owe a debt of gratitude to the pioneers of photography for developing tools that connected with our group and individual psyches. In this regard, the history of photography is integrally related to our passion for modern photography.

Lifestyle versus Art

Is photography your life? Or is it something you do when the inspiration strikes? Are you like a hobby painter who sits down at the easel once in a while to work with brushes and canvas? Or do you breathe, drink and eat with photography in your body and soul all the time? Do you spend many nights on photography websites looking at images and cameras, or do you just read Popular Photography once a month? Neither is good or bad, or right or wrong.

A painter may meditate for inspiration and perhaps make written notes during her waking hours. Eventually she will sit down and start her concept or vision. Similarly, a photographer who lives the passion all the time might carry some kind of camera with him. A painter, too, might take a camera frequently to record a scene or inspiration, putting it on paper or canvas later, but that's not to imply that it's the same thing. The real question here is whether you view your dreams or spend your waking hours consumed by photography and all of its elements - art, vision, processes, equipment, software. Is it lifestyle versus occasional art?

Are You a Craftsman or an Artist?

Since the early 19th century, modern photography has been seen as a craft. A photographer recorded images of scenes, events, and live subjects. While good or great photography has always required talent, that talent was considered derived from the expertise of the craft.

The price of entry into the photography field was high, in terms of cost, time and dedication. Very specialized knowledge was required to manipulate a view camera, and more importantly, to process wet plates, film and prints. Making good prints required considerable time and experience.

Great photography today requires expertise with the craft and knowledge of the digital tools, including the most sophisticated cameras, as well as powerful computers and amazing software. All of them are more and more available to the general public. That makes me wonder, where was the artist over the last two centuries and when did photography become a fine art? More importantly, what makes an image fine art or collectible material?

History has played an important part in turning photography into art. The simple aging of many wonderful photographs never intended as art has made them collectibles. Once that began to happen, many photographers began creating photography as art, and the 19th and 20th centuries gave us many names that we consider artists because of their successful efforts to create photography as art. A few examples include John Edwin Mayall, Ansel Adams, Diane Arbus, Julia Margaret Cameron, Alfred Stieglitz, Edward Steichen, Sally Mann, Edward Weston, Tina Modotti and Robert Mapplethorpe, among many others.

Modern collectors have converted many photographs published for other purposes into fine art. The most obvious examples are from the fields of photojournalism, advertising and fashion. Original prints by photographers like Henri Cartier-Bresson and Richard Avedon hold onto substantial value. In later decades, portraits intended as private commissions also became fine art.

If you want to be called an artist, is art defined by the type of work you do? An artistic portrait photographer may be perceived differently from a mainstream studio photographer. Many brilliant, lucky or classic world event images become fine art photographs for collectors, yet this was not the intention of the photographer at the time. A Pulitzer Prize winning image does not automatically become fine art. Only the passing of time may decide that the photograph is a collectible. And collectible does not necessarily define "art".

Over the decades, nudes have been the subject of many artists who have created their photographs only for the aesthetic art. Of course, nudes in painting and sculpture have been popular with artists for many centuries, if not thousands of years. Beautifully executed glamour and boudoir photography today is very artistic in the hands of the right photographer. Art in photography is not limited to film. Since digital photography became the norm, some amazing work has been created. But can or does privately commissioned photography ever become accepted or collected as fine art? It has been proven that it is a matter of time, and also uniqueness. Photoshop and filtering software have resulted in millions of similar, albeit spectacular, images whose style was quite homogenous. As always, a few photographers with true originality or personal style will stand the test of time and perhaps become collectible.

Commercially, all photography has always been considered a craft. Selectively, it has become an art for certain photographs, intentionally or unintentionally. If you have studied and learned the techniques of photography and you know your equipment, you are a craftsman. You may also be an artist, if you use your camera and produce your photographs in an artistic way. You are an artist if you have a special talent that produces photographs of an artistic nature. You may become famous if your art is unique.

If you are not yet a great artist it does not mean you are not an artist. Many artists have been late bloomers in finding their calling as adults, or even later in life. Perhaps you have not developed your talent enough yet to become a good artist. You have decided to create images using a camera, and that by itself can give you the potential for developing as an artist.

The same philosophy will apply to an acrylic painter, a watercolorist or a sculptor. Each has the necessary tools and raw materials, and when they begin using them they can become an artist. However, in their first week they may not be able to produce anything with finish or any work that appeals to someone wishing to decorate their home or collect for pleasure and profit. Of course, art and beauty are in the eye of the beholder. A lot of mediocre photography is sold at art fairs, along with some spectacular works of art.

Even if you are born a natural artist, full of talent and imagination, you will still need time to learn to use the tools of your chosen medium. With either the traditional tools of classic art or the tools of photography, an artist requires time to develop into a skillful craftsperson. How long it takes depends on the medium and how natural the process is adapted to the individual artist. Painting comes naturally to many people, yet others struggle to produce anything but immature works. The same can happen with sculpting and photography.

Some might argue that in its crudest form, relying solely on the camera's automatic function, any person can point the camera at a subject, the sensor will record a reasonably accurate image, and the subsequently viewable image or print could be art, voila, just like that. Others will counter that such a photograph will purely be a lucky shot. Who is right?

By the same logic of thought, a painter may argue that she is an artist by the simple act of splattering a few colors on a canvas. Very modern, very abstract, yet unique. She could also argue that it took talent to pre-visualize the final painting and create it, that not everyone can duplicate what she did on the canvas, simple as it may look. Is she right? Would that be enough to consider her an artist?

So are you a craftsperson or an artist? History has proven that you have to develop your craft before your work will develop into art. First comes the training, then the individual vision, then your unique works. The length of the process is different for each photographer.

For Money or For Love?

This may be the most important question photographers have been asking themselves for decades. Even in the early days of Kodak box cameras, when personal empowerment first unleashed the passion for many amateurs, photographers had to decide whether to enjoy the fun of photography or consider becoming a professional. Thousands of new photographers now try to become professionals every year, fueled by today's ease of discovering the passion of photography through digital cameras. If professional simply means charging for a photograph, anyone can become a pro, but it does not automatically mean photographic expertise, although it certainly implies it, as it should.

With the influx of new photographers into the business, and its massive, resulting competition, will anyone be able to make a living with photography? What would set you apart from the other tens of thousands of new professional photographers? Are you willing to dedicate long hours to becoming an expert craftsperson and to developing your own style? And are you a good businessman or businesswoman? As thousands of photographers attempt to become professionals, the vast majority also go out of business, discovering it is, indeed, a very difficult business. The main reasons for not surviving in the business are: running out of operating capital before viable, consistent revenues are realized; not charging enough for assignments, prints and albums; not having a clue as to their revenues and expenses; clients not being sufficiently impressed with the work; and poor customer service and poor quality photography. Those who have closed their doors invariable admit that this business is very difficult, and not really that much fun other than the shooting.

A very important question that you should ask yourself is, do you really want to take photographs *for* others? Many who have tried the professional photography life and get out have discovered that they are much happier as an amateur photographer, choosing their preferred subjects and enjoying their own work. When shooting for love and passion the art evolves differently. When photography is a business one may want to go home and do something else at the end of their day. Then there is the fact no one ever tells them that in this business there frequently is no "end of your day". For an independent photographer without a staff there are usually many long nights dedicated to post production. This, of course, is a byproduct of digital photography. Professional photographers before digital simply sent the film and print orders to a lab. Today most digital photographers have to do on the computer what the labs used to take care of for film photographers.

There are other avenues for making money in photography that do no entail private commissions for portraits, weddings, commercial ads, illustration, photojournalism, modeling portfolios, or tabletop photos.

First there is the art show circuit and related activities. You spend your free time shooting subjects that not only appeal to you, but also that your target market will like for decor. Subjects can include landscapes, both near your home base and those you take while on the road. Other popular subjects are horses, dogs, cats, fruits, and other still life subjects. In short, what sells paintings at art shows can also sell photographs. Large canvases are popular, as well as smaller, mounted prints of the same images. Most work tends to be in color and realistic. Some photographers have found a lucrative art show market by dedicating time to "painting" their color images using either Adobe Photoshop or Corel Painter. By printing them on canvas gallery wraps or on fine art paper the illusion is accomplished and the prints can bring in a lucrative price.

Then there is the fine art market. The target client is the collector of fine art photography. While dominated by black & white prints, there is some demand for color prints. Fine art black & white prints can range in selling price from a few hundred to several thousand dollars, depending on the impact and quality of the photograph or the fame of the photographer. Technically, fine art photography requires a highly dedicated level of perfection. Not only must good planning and great care be taken in shooting the image, but post production must be of the highest quality. Some fine art photographers perfect their images with software and then output their prints on special papers using their own printers. Other photographers still use darkroom techniques to produce prints using traditional methods, including gelatin. And as noted before, there are still master printers and fine art labs who can deliver to you incredible, museum quality, collectible prints.

Finally, there is the stock photography market. Images of almost any subject may be in demand by publishers looking to buy images for their websites or publications. Although stock photographers can sell their images on their own gallery websites, stock agencies are in the business of connecting buyers to photographers. Any photographer can create and upload stock images to sell, but there are some who dedicate their time to creating stock images. This can entail having a camera handy and shooting things as you go, or shooting a scene with models to create a concept that might be in demand by buyers. Stock photography was once a highly lucrative avenue, mostly reserved for photographers having established relationships with important stock agencies. While some exclusive agencies of the old model still exist, today there are popular stock websites with tens of thousands of photographers and millions of images. Prices for use of images have also plummeted from hundreds and thousands of dollars per use, to single digit dollars for practically unlimited use. You can shoot what pleases you, and upload the ones you wish to license.

Many a photographer who becomes a slave to his business will tell you that they wish they could photograph only for fun and personal satisfaction. On the other hand, many will tell you that they would rather suffer in the photography business than return to a boring job working for someone else or doing something else.

It would be remiss not to mention that there are corporate and government photography jobs with good salaries. And in the academic world there are photography teaching jobs for those well qualified. Top photographers in their field also give back to the profession by offering seminars and workshops, and some make a good supplemental income from speaking and teaching. Doing seminars and workshops can be a double edge sword, however, as many instructors will tell you that their photography business suffers when they spend too much time teaching.

As far as fun and personal photography, camera clubs are thriving everywhere with amateur photographers who love to shoot, print, share, and enter contests among their club peers. Much of the photography is quite spectacular, being a combination of skill and love. They have time, energy, a good attitude, and a passion to create their best. They are well rewarded by their clubs and their friends.

So, for money or for love?

Inspiration and the Muse

Where does your inspiration for personal photography come from? Do you simply take a camera, head off into the streets on your day off and see what there is to photograph? This can be one relaxing and rewarding way to spend a day. While opportunities are everywhere, and many great photographs have been taken like this over the years, it is similar to a novelist making up the story as she goes along. No planning. Pure serendipity. While the approach may have seemingly low-yielding results, great street photographers like Cartier-Bresson did exactly that. But they have admitted that they also ended up with many images destined for the trash. If you have suffered disappointments with this approach or wasted too much time, then perhaps some work on planning may reinvigorate your imagination. Like storyboarding a movie, planning a photograph concept can be very rewarding.

To be completely original you need to clear your mind and use your imagination to create a concept. Form your idea or ideas, then plan and execute the resulting assignment. For originality, your concept must come from your mind, but you can draw inspiration from your surroundings.

So what about a muse? There are actually several types of muses. One is the live muse, as enjoyed by many photographers over the decades. Most famously, the muse has been a woman inspiring a male photographer. She has served in some cases as the model who not only brings out the best in him, but has also been the subject of the photographs. Some photographers have had muses like a wife for inspiration, but paid models were the actual subjects. It also should be mentioned that some female photographers in history also had live muses for inspiration.

Another, and more common, type of muse is the imaginary or spiritual muse. Such a muse works through your mind, spirit or soul and gives you the fresh ideas you need to create original works. The questions is, how do we get in touch with this muse?

One way is through meditation, which can clear the mind of the modern clutter we carry with us. Clutter includes thinking about other events of the day, plans for tomorrow, emails and social network posts, meals or snacks, pets and children needing attention. The list can be endless. Meditation can help you clear the clutter and focus you on the relaxation needed. Only through imagination can we create something truly exciting, worthwhile and unique. If formal meditation does not appeal to you, you can simply find a quiet place and start visualizing. First, visualize total relaxation and clear all thoughts from your mind. Then think only of new ideas, writing them down quickly as they come to you. Let the mind flow freely. Let the muse awaken and take over your head. You will be amazed by the ideas that flow under those conditions. Make a list of all the ideas that come to you, never ignoring an idea. Then go back and treat each idea individually, encouraging it and letting it grow larger. It is not an easy process, but very rewarding. A lot of practice will be required to be able to jump from free thought to writing down ideas and back to free thought. You may lose a few thoughts along the way, but this will be unavoidable until someone invents a way to record what goes through your mind.

The muse can also inspire new ideas for professional photographers, many of whom do amazing work for their clients. A photographer needs time to relax, think, and let the imagination flow. Perhaps it is more difficult for professional photographers, who can suffer from a larger number of distractions, including a bombardment of images from everywhere. I would argue that a muse-based imagination is actually crucial for the professional photographer. But it is difficult to be original when under pressure. Only through the flow of new ideas can she create, develop and evolve a style that sets her apart from the competition, and that gives clients reasons to return for more. The muse and the imagination are not only important for creating new concepts, but also to see the aha moments that apply to the styling of the project, session or assignment. Herein can lie your unique selling attributes.

Whether you photograph private clients, commercial jobs, journalism, stock, or fine art, let the muse sizzle your imagination and infuse fresh ideas into your work. Make it a lifetime habit.

The Photographer's Mastermind Group

If one mind can meditate and create a new idea, many minds working together can develop a concept with even more power. Throughout history, friends or colleagues with a mutual interest or goal have gotten together to think and they have created powerful ideas together. Napoleon Hill, who studied successful people all of his life, decades ago popularized the concept of creating a group of like-minded persons with whom to meet frequently and brainstorm. Through many examples, he demonstrated the power of combining minds with others. There is a certain magic that happens when the imagination of two or more are united to work on an idea. Where the muse can stimulate the mind of one person through quiet thinking, the mastermind group can accomplish a similar effect by a simple meeting of the minds. In both scenarios, creativity runs freely.

Historically, photographers, painters and other artists have gotten together regularly to enjoy a drink, a meal, and discuss each others' projects and ideas. Many well known photographers have been friends, spending time in each other's homes and studios and finding inspiration from the work of their contemporaries. Equally, they could evolve ideas just by sitting somewhere quietly focusing on a concept.

Today there are meetings at associations for professional photographers, camera clubs for amateurs, and a multitude of seminars and conventions, where inspiration, learning and training are the plan. Some photographers still make time to meet in smaller groups with special colleagues or friends that share the same interests.

The Internet and social media sites also created places where photographers can meet for ideas and inspiration, including groups for specific topics. There you can find groups that view and discuss images taken by specific cameras. There are groups that discuss portrait photography and other specialties. There are groups who meet regularly to go on photo shoots. While these photo shoots may not bring you money or prestige, the benefit comes from learning ideas and techniques from other members. Meet-ups have sprouted like mushrooms everywhere, bringing together photographers with similar interests.

My top recommendation would be to carefully create your own private face to face group of photographers, those whom you find truly inspiring. Try to meet a few times a year in your private homes. Plan relaxing dinners and have great open conversations about the art. Have each member invite a like-minded photographer from time to time. This is how strong artist relationships are formed.

When you join formal organizations, do so with groups who include time for networking and sharing, not just structured lectures. Go to conventions and to convention dinners and parties. You will make new, life-lasting friends. You will later wonder how you ever got along without them.

The Fallacies of the Equipment Beliefs

"What camera do you use?" is a common question from would be photographers. Do you immediately tell the innocent questioner what's in your camera bag, or do you try to shift the conversation to the techniques of your work? That common question can be annoying because an experienced photographer knows that she can create beautiful images with any camera. "What camera do you use?" Indeed. Are photographers just looking for validation or do they need a mentor to help choose their next camera system?

Too many new photographers, and the general public, believe that a great camera or an inadequate camera make the stunning image or the lousy shot. Of course, nothing could be further from the truth.

Experienced painters know that their choices in brushes do not pave the road to great art. While great brushes and paint, like a superb lens, are a tremendous asset, they know that what will make their work special is their talent and taking the concept from their mind to their hand. So, why do photographers get into the equipment trap? Why does the camera give them a false empowerment, blind to the wisdom of the watercolor artist? Shouldn't a great photograph also begin with a concept in the mind, followed by craft and talent, then by well-learned software techniques? The combination of a great camera/lens and imaging software will not automatically produce a masterpiece.

Let's examine another art form that is also photography - the motion picture. The story is the product of someone's mind, whether the author of a novel, an original screenwriter, or a director who chooses the writer. The final script is given to another type of artist who sketches a storyboard. A director of photography takes the storyboards and plans the shots and lighting with the film's director. Many decisions are made, resulting in choices of film, camera, lens, lighting, focus, and more, multiplied by the number of scenes. Actors, photographer, director, crew and post production staff then work and follow a plan to make the original concept appear on film. Why should the process of taking a single photograph be any different? Naturally, making a film is a far more complex and collaborative effort, but just the same, whether movie, photograph, or oil painting a concept must be taken from the mind to the the final creation.

In comparing the tools of photography and painting, they are similar in some respects, but quite the opposite in others. A photography enthusiast who wants to take great photos can go to an electronics retailer, buy any DSLR body and lens, and begin taking pretty decent photos. If he dedicates a lot of time, study and practice, he may discover and develop a talent for great photographic art.

A painting enthusiast may go to an art supply store, buy brush, paper and paint and set up at a quiet spot to begin painting. If we assume that they both have a sense of composition, the photographer will capture a scene with a simple click while the painter will need time for getting her idea down on the final paper or canvas.

The amateur painter starts out by looking at a blank sheet, finalizing an imagined concept of what to paint and what colors to use, along with how to properly manipulate the brushes and mix the colors. The amateur photographer will open his snapshot with the imaging software that came with his camera or her computer, or maybe will use a professional application, and with a little practice may convert the snapshot into a reasonably attractive and advanced image. He has editing tools and filters that today almost anyone can learn to use. The new painter must practice lines, directions, color, perspective of elements, and other factors. Possibly she might throw away a few papers before getting to a point where the painting is a keeper.

Chances are it will take the painter longer to achieve good skills, but less time to establish a personal style.

The new photographer can achieve decent skills with the camera, and with the right software. But the final image will look like that of many other photographers who are also fairly new to both the camera and digital imaging. Developing a personal style is a challenge that plagues both new photographers and seasoned ones, and a process that can take a lifetime.

In photography, it all starts in the photographer's mind, whether from a muse, meditation, an external inspiration, or a mastermind group. To paraphrase Napoleon Hill, "What the imagination creates, the mind can work to achieve".

So getting back to the original question, "What camera do you use?", the better question should be "How did you develop your craft and your style?" Every photographer, new and experienced, is interested in cameras and gear, and the benefits of one or another should be the subject of some lessons, but discussion of the art, and how to create it, is far more relevant to the growth of a photographer.

Passion, or healthy obsession?

At some point, or at many points, in your life you will ask yourself this question. Is photography a controlled part of my life, something I do for art, hobby, fun, or even profession? Or is photography a lifestyle that permeates everything I do? Is photography my expression of art, or a passion that encompasses everything from concepts and ideas to equipment and imaging tools? Do I get overloaded and have to "turn it off" once in a while, or do I love it so much that I don't mind that every waking or sleeping thought is photography? Do I go to bed every night reading my photography magazines and social network group discussions on my tablet? Can I turn it off and enjoy a movie once in a while? Or will I just analyze movies for their photography?

Does your life partner share in your photography passion, or is he an outsider to your photography life? Art, including photography, can be a lonely interest not shared to the same degree by your favorite person. This disparity can be problematic with any unshared interest or passion that either of you have. It is important in any close relationship for both parties to take an interest in each other's favorite activities. You will find your relationship more fulfilling if you can share your triumphs and accomplishments. It helps to be open and share your photography with her, but it will always be crucial to keep that person and your relationship in perspective, giving her the attention she deserves.

If you met this person when you already had a developed passion for photography, chances are you put your photography passion on the back burner while you fell in love. You were emotionally and physically passionate about, and with, your new love. To maintain a lifelong romance it can be important that your passion for that special person in your life never waver or become secondary to your passion for photography. A fulfilled partner will always understand, support, and help you with your other love - photography.

The flip side of living and breathing photography takes place on those occasions when you feel that perhaps you need a break. You may need a break from carrying a camera all the time, spending too much time online discussing equipment, reading too many books and magazines, and, the big one, spending too much time on the computer perfecting your images. Digital photography can become overwhelming on many levels and you will need a break from time to time. Will this mean that you no longer have a passion for photography? Not at all. It simply means that perhaps you overdid it. You overdosed, so to speak. Take a break. Sober up. Do something else. Find out what your family would like to do. Update other hobbies and read about other interests. Go spend more time on fun and health activities for a while. Eventually, inevitably, the photography passion will creep back in, slowly filling your veins as it did before.

When it does, you will recognize that the break was worth it and that you are once again full of energy and passion.

The New Passionate Photographers

Photography is a passion with a history. It is also a modern phenomenon of growing dimensions. During the 20th century the passion was much less prevalent, but it did exist and resulted in wonderful images now found in museums, art galleries and personal collections. There have always been photographers of all types with passions for taking images, for the equipment, for the smell of chemistry in the darkroom, and for the artistic creation that is a photograph.

In the 21st century, however, a new genesis group is evolving. Most photographers abandoned film photography and its lab-oriented or complicated darkroom process, and instead switched to digital cameras and software. Smartphones at one point diminished the interest in other cameras because of the sheer convenience of always carrying a combination camera/phone. At first the public found it reasonably easy to copy images from their memory card or phone to a computer. And while the printing of snapshots continued in popularity, the sharing paradigm quickly transitioned from passing out prints or emailing digital files, to uploading images to social networks.

The interesting phenomenon, however, is not fundamentally about printing or sharing. It is that a disproportionate and growing, number of people are becoming possessed with a passion for advanced photography. It's possible that they may have outgrown their point and shoot camera or they may have discovered cool image manipulating apps for their phone. Then suddenly they have found themselves engulfed in all things photography - magazines, Internet discussions, collections of amazing new work. They found a way to get in and participate. Many became convinced that a DSLR is a fundamental tool. First, the investment was justified because they expect to take great family photos, including those of the kids at soccer and other activities. Second, because they really needed better photos of their vacations. Third, because they were now "serious" about photography, with plans to either become superb artists or to become the professional photographer they feel they were meant to be.

So, who are you?

Are you a collector, street photographer, or family snap-shooter? Sometimes it can take months, or even years, to discover your specific photography passion. What is most important is the discovery process. Discovery can be collecting fine art prints and realizing that you needed to shoot some of those images yourself. Discovery can mean thoroughly enjoying your family snapshots and not wanting to do more than crop and adjust color on a few images. Discovery can be that you love shooting black & white photography and your favorite subject is life on the streets. Discovery for some has been going to a wedding, shadowing the professional photographer and realizing that they have to be one of them.

But the real passion this journey explores is the one found by some photographers, in which you become consumed by everything photography - news, books, equipment, technique, fine art, continuing education, and, for some, a profession for life. How much passion may not be a matter of degree, but of time. In other words, will you have the fever for a year or for a lifetime? Or will it come and go as you fight distractions from other facets of life. Only time can tell.

Why identify the passion and discuss it at all? Because if you are a consumed photographer you need to learn what to do with your photography and with your life. The passion itself should tell you, but it does not always. For some it can be a very confusing time, perhaps deciding between another career and a photography career, or between going to photography school and going law school. More importantly, how manageable will the passion be? Photography as an avocation can be expensive and time consuming. As a profession it can be brutally competitive and exhausting. Either way, too much photography can lead to burn-out. Photography is a beautiful thing, but not without perils.

Modern photography is a term that is decades old, yet now it has taken on a different meaning. It has also empowered the artist inside many people who can now express themselves through a visual medium that before was never truly user friendly. The tools available to all types of photographers will continue to evolve at a very rapid pace.

Follow your heart and your imagination. If you have read this far you know that you have a personal connection with your passion. Live it, express it, guide it, control it, and let photography be the reason you live an interesting life.